Your Start-Up Starts Now!
A Guide to Entrepreneurship

What Is Environmental Entrepreneurship?

Alexander Offord

Crabtree Publishing Company
www.crabtreebooks.com

Author: Alexander Offord

Series research and development: Reagan Miller

Editors: Helen Mason, Kathy Middleton

Proofreader: Renata Brunner Jass

Editorial services: Clarity Content Services

Project coordinator and prepress technician: Tammy McGarr

Print coordinator: Katherine Berti

Series consultant: Rebecca Darling

Cover design: Margaret Amy Salter

Design: David Montle

Photo Research: Linda Tanaka

Photo Credits:

Cover: All images from Shutterstock
Title page: CCL/TonyTheTiger; pp4-5 Starryboy/dreamstime; p5 Courtesy of Garden Pool; p6 left Courtesy of Scooter Clark, CCL/Padraic Ryan; p7 Photo courtesy of Interface Americas, Inc.; pp8-9 Courtesy of Wheelys Café; p10 CCL/Maurizio Pesce from Milan, Italia; p11 ssuaphotos/Shutterstock; p12 Copyright 1939 by H.H. Wittemann, Library of Congress, inset, Bundesarchiv_Bild_183-1990-1126-500, Kraftdroschke; p13 left AP Photo/The Canadian Press, Courtesy of Crotched Mountain Foundation; p14 Simikov/Shutterstock, inset, Michigan Sea Grant; p15 top CCL/J.M.Garg, Courtesy of Buckaroo Organics; p16 Travel Stock/Shutterstock; p17 top Courtesy of Bakeys, Courtesy of Peggy Cross; p18 Monkey Business Images/Shutterstock; p19 top Svetoslav Radkov/Shutterstock, Courtesy of Crobar; p20 TairA/Shutterstock; p21 top Photo courtesy of Green Sense Farms, Robert Colangelo, Founding Farmer, Courtesy of Plan Creations Co. Ltd.; p22 Svetlana Eremina/Shutterstock; p23 Courtesy of SustainEarth; p24 Courtesy Hydrostor; p25 Courtesy The Bioo Team, Arkyne Technologies; pp26-27 Courtesy of WakaWaka; p28 Whole Foods Market; p29 Balefire/Shutterstock; p30 Courtesy Freedom of Animals. Photo by Scott MacDonough; p31 Courtesy of Nanoleaf, bottom Courtesy of Tonya Kay. Photo by Melissa Schwartz. Retouch by Stephen Newell; p32 Carloscastilla/dreamstime, p33 top Courtesy Bullfrog Power Inc. and White Squall, Darren Brode/Shutterstock; p34 Lauren Hurley/PA Images/Alamy Stock Photo; p35 praisaeng/iStock; p36 top CCL/Erik (HASH) Hersman, Courtesy of The Ocean Cleanup; p37 top Courtesy of Zymal Umar/Zee Bags, Courtesy of Ecoviate, Photo: European Union Contest for Young Scientists; p38 Wally Stemberger/Shutterstock, BufferedBrain/Shutterstock; p39 Photo courtesy of YAY Bale Team; p40 stockphoto mania/Shutterstock; p41 robert mobley/Shutterstock; p42 Arend Trent/Shutterstock; p43 Tom Wang/Shutterstock.

t=Top, bl=Bottom Left, br=Bottom Right

Library and Archives Canada Cataloguing in Publication

Offord, Alexander, author
What is environmental entrepreneurship? / Alexander Offord.

(Your start-up starts now! a guide to entrepreneurship)
Includes bibliographical references and index.
Issued in print and electronic formats.
ISBN 978-0-7787-2756-9 (hardback).--
ISBN 978-0-7787-2764-4 (paperback).--ISBN 978-1-4271-1822-6 (html)

1. Sustainable development--Juvenile literature. 2. Social responsibility of business--Juvenile literature. 3. Small business--Environmental aspects--Juvenile literature. 4. Environmental economics--Juvenile literature. 5. Entrepreneurship--Juvenile literature. I. Title.

HD30.255.O34 2016 j658.4'083 C2016-903413-5 C2016-903414-3

Library of Congress Cataloging-in-Publication Data

Names: Offord, Alexander, author.
Title: What is environmental entrepreneurship? / Alexander Offord.
Description: New York : Crabtree Publishing, [2017] | Series: Your start-up starts now! A guide to entrepreneurship | Includes bibliographical references and index.
Identifiers: LCCN 2016026654 (print) | LCCN 2016038424 (ebook) | ISBN 9780778727569 (reinforced library binding) | ISBN 9780778727644 (pbk.) | ISBN 9781427118226 (Electronic HTML)
Subjects: LCSH: Green products--Juvenile literature. | Environmentalism--Juvenile literature. | Entrepreneurship--Juvenile literature. | New business enterprises--Juvenile literature.
Classification: LCC HD9999.G772 O44 2017 (print) | LCC HD9999.G772 (ebook) | DDC 658.4/083--dc23
LC record available at https://lccn.loc.gov/2016026654

Crabtree Publishing Company
www.crabtreebooks.com 1-800-387-7650

Printed in Canada/102016/IH20160811

Published in Canada
Crabtree Publishing
616 Welland Ave.
St. Catharines, Ontario
L2M 5V6

Published in the United States
Crabtree Publishing
PMB 59051
350 Fifth Avenue, 59th Floor
New York, New York 10118

Published in the United Kingdom
Crabtree Publishing
Maritime House
Basin Road North, Hove
BN41 1WR

Published in Australia
Crabtree Publishing
3 Charles Street
Coburg North
VIC, 3058

Contents

The World of Tomorrow

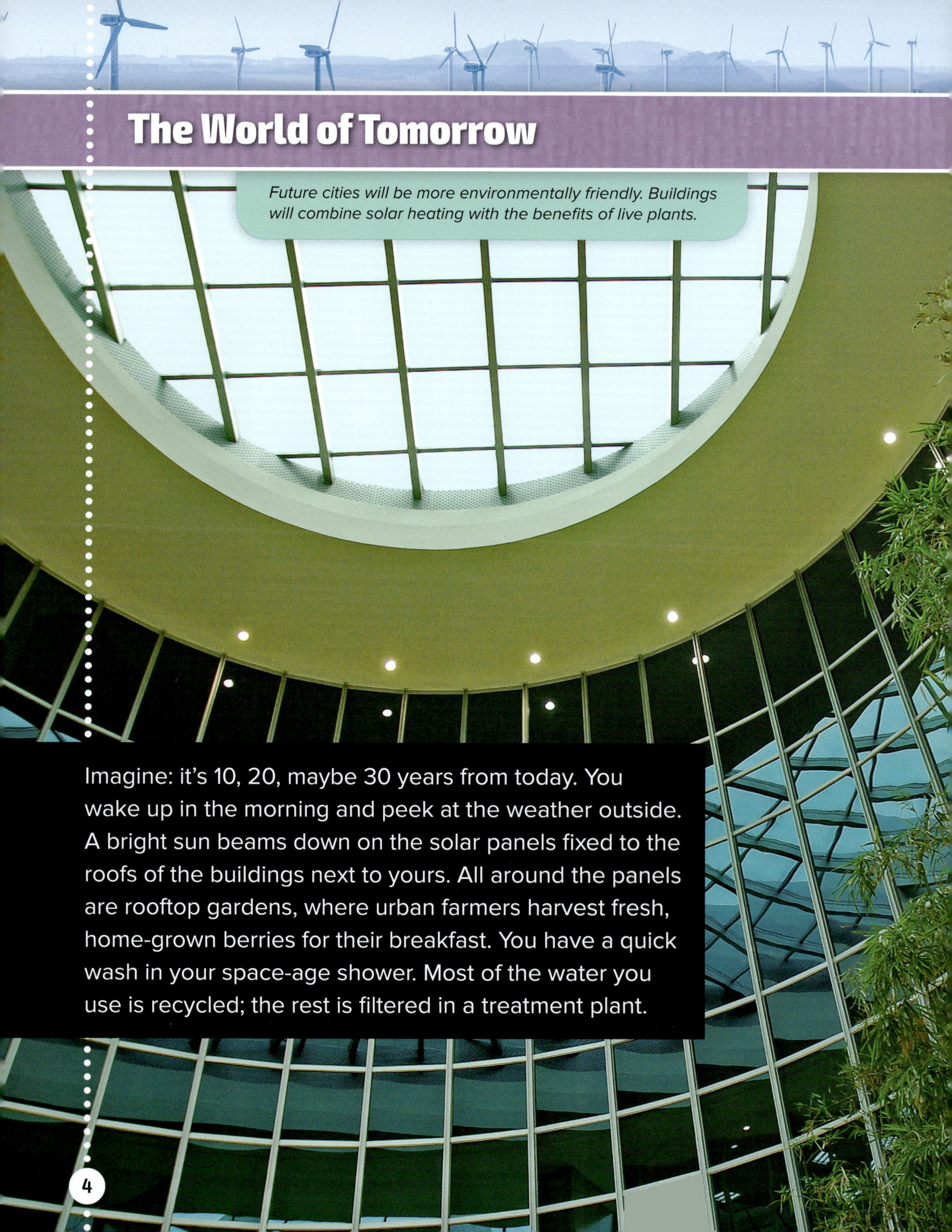

Future cities will be more environmentally friendly. Buildings will combine solar heating with the benefits of live plants.

Imagine: it's 10, 20, maybe 30 years from today. You wake up in the morning and peek at the weather outside. A bright sun beams down on the solar panels fixed to the roofs of the buildings next to yours. All around the panels are rooftop gardens, where urban farmers harvest fresh, home-grown berries for their breakfast. You have a quick wash in your space-age shower. Most of the water you use is recycled; the rest is filtered in a treatment plant.

You get dressed and make breakfast using the fresh eggs your hens have laid overnight. Their small coop sits on the balcony. You compost their manure to use as fertilizer for your garden.

After eating, you unplug your smartphone from the USB port built directly into a potted plant. Overnight, **photosynthesis**, which occurs in the plant, has recharged the battery. You glance at the time: you're running late!

Usually you would hop on the high-speed electric train that takes you right into the city. Today, you get in your electric car and take off down the road. The road you drive on is made of special solar panels. Together with the rows of windmills on the horizon, these panels power the entire city.

You breathe deep as you rocket along the highway, windows rolled down. The breeze smells fresh because the paint on the buildings you whip by is specially designed to react with water droplets and sunlight to pull pollution from the air.

This is just a glimpse of the world of tomorrow. It is a world in which **environmental entrepreneurship** has created a cleaner, healthier planet. It is a world that celebrates the best of both high-tech modern conveniences and traditional ways of life. It is a world where technology and the environment exist in harmony. The world of tomorrow is actually being built right now by environmental **entrepreneurs**.

For some, the future is already here. This sketch shows the Garden Pool, an Arizona-based ecohome started by the McClung family. They raise chickens, vegetables, and fish in what used to be a swimming pool. The home is solar-powered, and all waste is recycled for fertilizer or food for the fish.

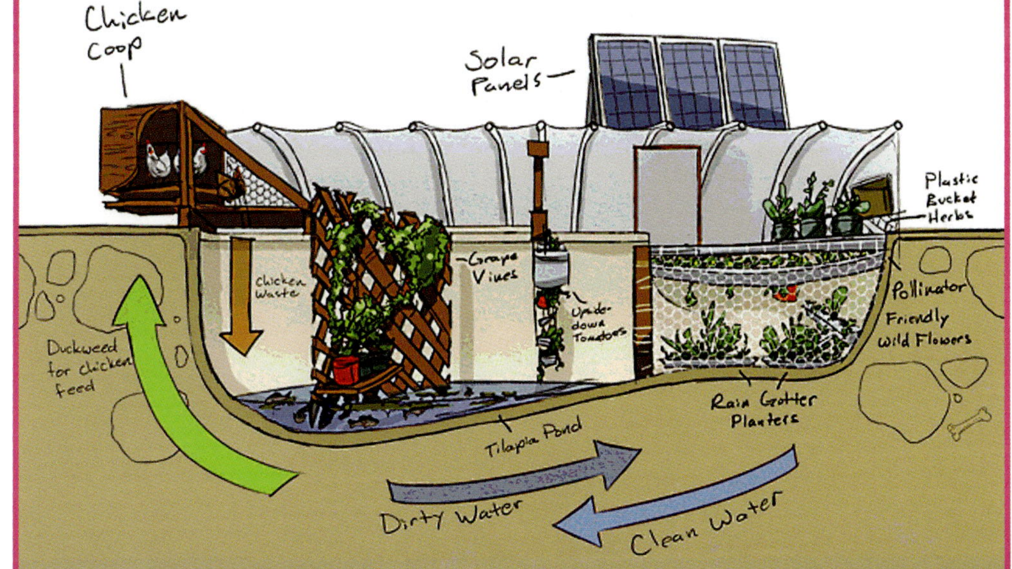

1 Where Innovation Meets Conservation

Entrepreneurship is the process of turning an idea into a business. The person at the head of this process is the entrepreneur. This is the person who will benefit—or lose—the most financially. Entrepreneurs also benefit by achieving a personal sense of satisfaction about their accomplishments.

Each summer, hundreds of workers brave the Canadian wilderness to plant trees. It's hard work, but there are many rewards, including good wages and a new forest.

Think of entrepreneurs as "doers" and "makers." They believe strongly in their product or service, and are willing to take risks in order to develop them and start new businesses. An entrepreneur is usually his or her own boss, the owner of his or her own company, and a unique and creative thinker.

Being an entrepreneur requires good organization, leadership, and planning skills, as well as an inventive mind. It also takes a lot of work. The good news is that there are no rules about who can be an entrepreneur. You can be an entrepreneur and change the world—without even leaving your home!

There are many kinds of entrepreneurship, including environmental, **social**, and **digital entrepreneurship**. An entrepreneur's personal passion determines what field they end up in. Environmental entrepreneurs—also called **ecopreneurs**—set out to solve environmental issues, such as **climate change**, species extinction, and wastefulness, using new and creative solutions. They find ways to earn money while also helping the environment, but money is not their main motivation.

*Nearly half of the **consumers** around the world are willing to pay extra for environmentally friendly products.*

Credit: Nielsen

Ray C. Anderson: Pioneer Ecopreneur

Ray Anderson was a pioneer of ecopreneurship. In 1973, he founded Interface, a company that makes carpet tiles for offices. At first he didn't worry about the environment. That changed in 1994 when he read a book called *The Ecology of Commerce* that encouraged caring for the environment when considering business practices. What he learned caused him to change his entire business model. Today, Interface uses renewable solar and wind energy, avoids toxic chemicals, and reduces waste by recycling.

It takes courage to change your way of doing business. Ray Anderson did just that after reading a book that explains how to make money and protect the environment.

You make the call...

Think of someone in your life that is a "doer" or a "maker." What makes them stand out? Do they have any qualities that you admire? Explain your thinking.

Willingness to take risks

In 2012, Marie de la Croix was the art director for an award-winning Swedish advertising agency, Studio Total. She took the big risk of quitting her job because she wanted to start an eco-friendly company. In 2015, she and former co-worker Tomas Mazetti started a company called Wheelys.

Wheelys is a company that allows individual entrepreneurs to start their own café-on-wheels. Their all-in-one bicycle coffee carts use only energy from the Sun and from the ***vendor's*** *pedaling.*

A year later, 378 Wheelys coffee-bikes were operating in 55 countries around the world, including Sweden, Canada, and the United States. Although things worked out for de la Croix, nothing was guaranteed. If the bikes hadn't sold, she would have been left in debt and without an **income**. Taking risks is necessary in entrepreneurship. The key is to make calculated risks. A calculated risk is one that has been researched and considered carefully, so that the outcome is more likely to be positive.

Vision

The founders of Wheelys had a strong vision. They wanted to provide quality **organic** coffee and snacks in an environmentally **sustainable** way, all around the world. That meant grinding the beans by hand and using solar panels to heat the coffee.

Perseverance

According to Marie de la Croix, the first year of Wheelys was a financial failure. The idea interested a lot of people but didn't make a **profit**. As a result, half of the original team quit. But, like all successful ecopreneurs, she was determined to figure out what had gone wrong and how to fix it. She teamed up with Y Combinator, a company that advises entrepreneurs and gives **start-up funds** to help new companies get off the ground. With their help, Wheelys began to grow.

Independence

Wheelys bikes allow anyone to be an entrepreneur. Entrepreneurs who buy a Wheelys bike are given the tools to run a business, but are responsible for hitting the streets themselves and selling the coffee. All entrepreneurs have to be independent enough to stay focused on the tasks at hand and move their company forward.

" We did extensive testing, building, and branding of the bikes in order to finally see an increase of the revenue [sales] by more than 50%. "

—Marie de la Croix,
CEO, Wheelys

When she ran into problems, Marie de la Croix found a way to solve them.

The Ecopreneurs

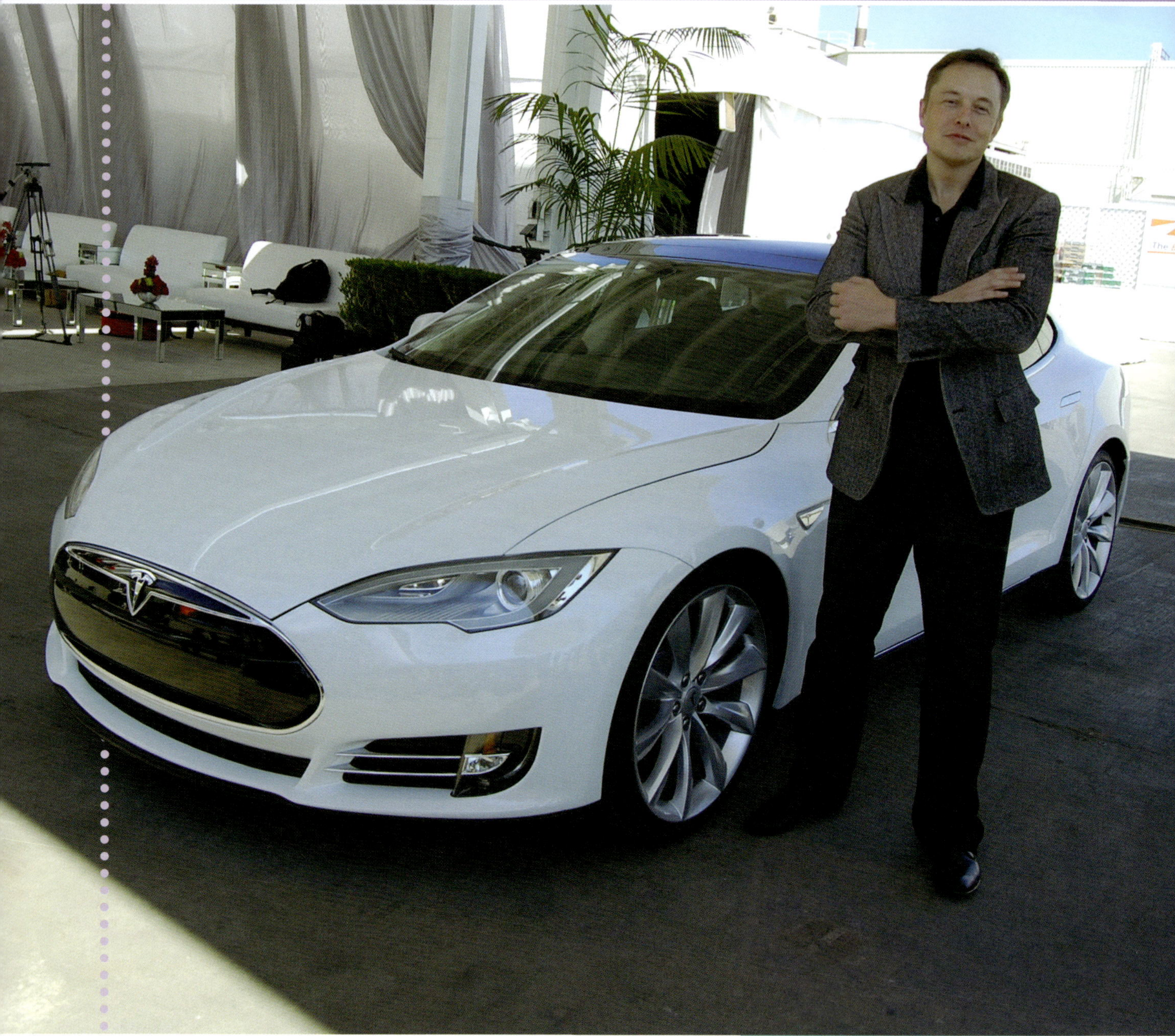

Green businesses try to reduce the demand on natural resources by using recycled materials and natural ingredients. They also try to reduce their use of non-renewable resources such as fossil fuels.

Elon Musk, founder of Tesla Motors, is one of the most successful ecopreneurs in the world. In 2016, he was worth $13 billion.

Burning fossil fuels such as gas, coal, and oil creates **greenhouse gases**, including **carbon dioxide (CO_2)**. These gases trap the Sun's heat, warming Earth above its normal average temperature. This warming effect leads to climate change, which can cause extreme droughts, wildfires, and floods. Usually, plants and natural processes remove plenty of carbon dioxide from the air. The problem is that human technology creates too much of it.

Elon Musk hopes to solve this problem. Born in South Africa, he is one of the most famous ecopreneurs in the world. At first, his interest in computers and software led him to found a software company called Zip2. Later he developed PayPal, an **innovative** online payment company. Thanks to these businesses, Musk was a millionaire by his late 20s.

But his passion goes far beyond money. He is also genuinely interested in making the world a greener place. Musk wants to eliminate greenhouse gas emissions from cars by replacing gas-powered engines with those that run on electric batteries. Most car engines run on gasoline, which is made from oil. Musk co-founded Tesla Motors in an effort to make affordable electric cars that travel faster and farther on renewable energy than his competitors' cars.

Musk is not afraid to dream big. He is also chairman of Solar City, a solar panel producer that intends to bring solar energy to homes across North America. Under another one of his pioneering companies, called SpaceX, Musk plans to colonize Mars! He believes this would ease some of the burden on Earth's natural resources.

*Three industries are responsible for most of the greenhouse gases that cause **global warming**—electricity and heat production, agriculture and forestry, and manufacturing.*

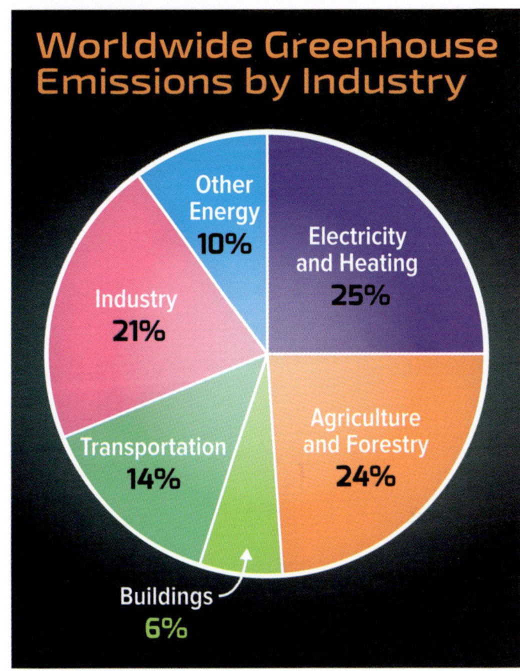

Credit: IPCC (2014).

Some scientists estimate that air pollution, such as car exhaust, contributes to 3.3 million deaths worldwide, each year.

The History of "Going Green"

By the late 1800s, gas-powered cars were quickly becoming popular. American politician William C. Whitney had another idea. What if he started a taxi company using only battery-powered vehicles? By 1900, there were more electric cars in New York City than cars powered by gasoline.

As early as the 1890s, electric taxis were beginning to replace horse-drawn carriages.

On October 4, 1955, the first solar-powered phone call was placed. All modern solar panels are based on the same design.

The Crotched Mountain wind farm had only 20 turbines. Today, wind farms can have hundreds or even thousands of turbines.

As the popularity of Whitney's company grew, the number of electric taxis increased. The taxis needed two batteries: one for driving and a spare that could be charged while the other one was being used. But batteries were expensive to maintain and manufacture, and Whitney soon began to lose money. At the same time, an oil boom in the United States had made gasoline cheaper and more available than ever. People didn't yet know about the dangers of air pollution from burning gasoline in cars. They weren't willing to pay extra for an electric taxi. As a result, Whitney's Electric Vehicle Company went bankrupt in 1907.

It wasn't until 1962 that people first became concerned about pollution. That year, an environmentalist named Rachel Carson published *The Silent Spring*. Her book highlighted the deaths of birds caused by pesticides. For the first time, the public was asked to consider the dangers of pumping chemicals and toxins into the environment.

Meanwhile, inventors were already working on sustainable technology. In 1954, three American scientists invented a special solar cell. Daryl Chapin, Calvin Fuller, and Gerald Pearson made their cell from silicon. The cell used a chemical reaction to turn sunlight into electricity. It was the first solar cell that could create a significant amount of energy.

Other renewable energy sources, such as wind power, have been used for much longer. In 1850, Daniel Halladay and John Burnham founded the U.S. Wind Engine Company. They sold windmills for use on farms in the American West. In 1980, the world's first **wind farm** was built at Crotched Mountain, New Hampshire.

2 The Mind of an Entrepreneur

The many problems of pollution and climate change cannot be fixed with only one solution. The environmental movement first started inside people's homes. People started recycling and reusing to reduce waste. Later, conserving resources such as water became a concern. Then people started finding ways to create products with ingredients that would not be harmful to people and to the environment.

Phosphorus encourages the growth of tiny plants called "algae." Large amounts of algae in a body of water use up the dissolved oxygen. Aquatic plants and animals that depend on oxygen die.

It is the same for **entrepreneurs**. Successful entrepreneurs begin, not by solving all of the world's problems, but by asking themselves, "What's my problem?" They keep their focus simple and specific. Lindsay and Brad Herron, a married couple from Montana, didn't set out to solve all the problems of pollution and climate change. Instead, they asked a few simple questions: "How can we, as a family, make better health-conscious choices? How can we teach our children about giving back? And how can we make a difference in the world?"

They realized that many of the products they used every day contained harmful, non-environmentally friendly ingredients. For example, many laundry detergents contain a chemical called **phosphorus**. When cleaning clothes, phosphorus helps break up dirt and grease. When the wastewater drains into lakes and rivers, however, phosphorus creates environmental problems.

In 2014, the Herrons founded Buckaroo Organics. Using Brad Herron's background as a chemist, they created their own soaps and ointments from natural, organic ingredients. Among other eco-friendly products, they sell a detergent made from the fruit of soapberry trees. The dried shells or nuts of the soapberry tree act as a natural soap. The berries contain no phosphorus. They do not harm lakes and rivers.

To make a difference in the world, the Herrons also started a Give5 Save5 program. Online shoppers who use the code "Save5" at the Buckaroo checkout save 5 percent on their purchases. In addition, the company donates 5 percent of the sale to a non-profit organization that works to bring safe drinking water to children around the world.

Soap nuts are a fruit of the Chinese soapberry tree. For centuries, people in India and other parts of Asia have used them to wash clothes. Many people who are allergic to detergent are not bothered by soapberries.

You make the call...

Think about an environmental problem in your home, school, or community. How might you be able to solve that problem? For example, are there ways to turn the things that people normally waste into something useful? Can you start a composting program? Or use scraps of paper in artwork?

Instead of phosphorus, soapberries contain a natural foaming chemical called saponin, which can clean clothing fibers.

Old Problem, New Approach

In New Delhi alone, there are an estimated 200,000 food vendors.

The true ecopreneur looks at problems and tries to imagine solutions that are different from the usual way of approaching a situation. Large cities in India, for example, have a problem that requires a unique solution. A culture of street food has developed that is celebrated by food-lovers from around the world. But it has a downside. These on-the-go diners use and dispose of a large number of plastic utensils. Although plastic spoons, knives, and forks can be recycled, less than 10% are. About 50%, or half, end up in landfills. The rest litter the streets. Many of these make their way to the ocean, where they threaten wildlife. Plastic utensils are dangerous both when they're whole and when they break up into small sharp pieces that can damage the internal organs of animals that consume them.

Narayana Peesapaty was a consultant who worked with farmers to create healthy crops. He also spent time studying forests. Thanks to his knowledge of plants and their uses, he thought of a solution that is so clever it makes you wonder why no one thought of it before.

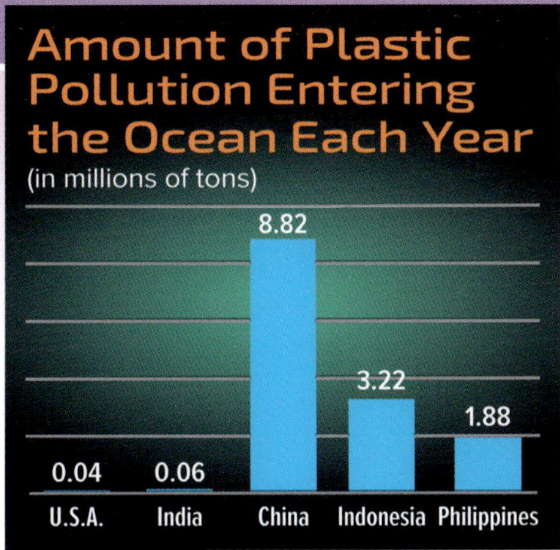

Credit: http://science.sciencemag.org/content/347/6223/768

In 2010, Peesapaty founded Bakeys Edible Cutlery. He uses sorghum flour to make edible utensils. Consumers can enjoy their meal—and then eat the cutlery. If they don't, it will **decompose** within four to five days. By 2016, Peesapaty's company was selling 1.5 million utensils a year.

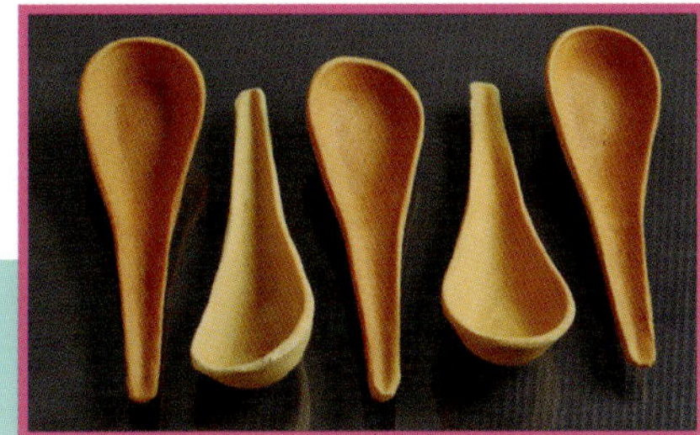

Peesapaty's utensils come in plain, sweet, salty, and spicy flavors.

Peggy Cross:
Innovative Ecopreneur

Before starting her own business, Peggy Cross was the creative director of a firm that designed packaging for foods and beverages. In 2010, she was packing a lunch for her children and couldn't find a spoon. That's when she had the idea for her EcoTensil: a compostable and recyclable cardboard utensil. Her first product, SpoonLidz, is both a lid and a spoon. Since then, the company has sold millions of eco-friendly forks and spoons all over the world.

Peggy Cross's EcoTensils are one-fifth the size of wooden or plastic utensils. This makes them easy to ship and store.

Do It Differently

Sometimes solutions already exist, but we have to change attitudes to make them work. For example, beef is a staple food in North America. Technologies developed over the past 100 years have allowed beef farmers to increase the amount of meat they produce. Unfortunately, common farming practices put more carbon dioxide (CO_2) into the atmosphere than all forms of transportation combined. This is due both to the energy used to grow the food the animals eat, and the gasoline used to transport the meat from farms to stores. Amazingly, the burps from cows also contribute to global warming.

When cows burp, they release **methane**, which is a greenhouse gas. Studies have shown that one cow can release the equivalent of four tons (3.6 metric tons) of CO_2 a year. There are currently about 1.5 billion cows being raised around the world. That's the equivalent of six billion tons (5.4 billion metric tons) of CO_2 each year.

In 2015, Americans bought 4.6 billion pounds (2.1 billion kilograms) of hamburger meat.

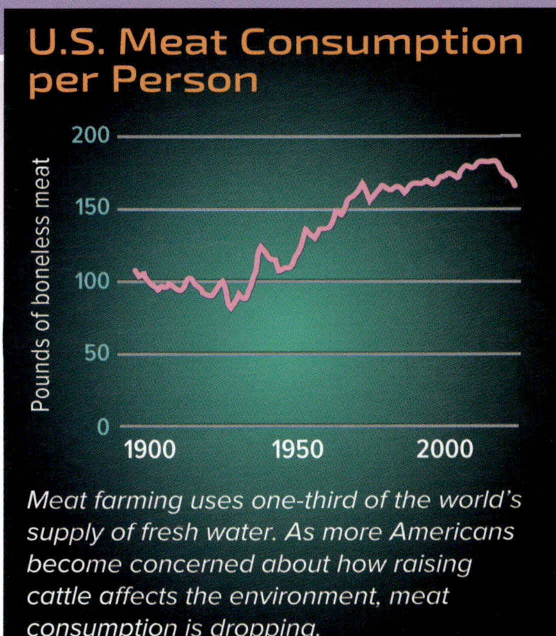

Meat farming uses one-third of the world's supply of fresh water. As more Americans become concerned about how raising cattle affects the environment, meat consumption is dropping.

Danish ecopreneur Christine Spliid wanted to help address the problem. But instead of trying to decrease the cows' CO_2, she developed a new food as an alternative to hamburger. In 2014, she created a way to give people protein without polluting the environment. Her food uses insects!

Most North Americans and Europeans consider eating insects "gross." But people in 80% of the world's countries regularly eat bugs. Not only are they a great source of protein, they need far less space and resources to grow than cows do. Crickets can be raised in plastic tubs and fed almost anything, including table scraps and grain.

This protein bar is made from crickets and contains 10 grams of protein per 60 grams.

Spliid ground crickets into flour and mixed them with chocolate or peanuts to create a delicious protein bar. In 2016, her company, Gathrfoods, was planning to make products using mealworms.

Insects such as this cricket are a good source of protein.

> "It's all a matter of changing perceptions and trends. When sushi was introduced to the West 30 years ago, most people were disgusted with the idea of eating raw fish, but after the fish got wrapped with some avocado and cream cheese, people changed their minds."
>
> – Christine Spliid, Gathrfoods

3 From Idea to Reality

While no two entrepreneurs have exactly the same story, all entrepreneurs follow a similar **entrepreneurial process**.

IDEA
▼
RESEARCH
▼
BUSINESS PLAN
▼
FUNDING
▼
MARKETING

All entrepreneurs follow these steps, from having the first inkling of an idea for solving a problem to making it a reality.

The sap from the rubber tree is called latex. When mixed with an acid, liquid latex becomes solid.

1. The Idea

It all starts with identifying a problem. For example, in 1981, Thai ecopreneur Vitool Viraponsavan was concerned about pollution. Rubber is made from the sap of the rubber tree. These trees originated in South America but are now grown on farms throughout Asia, including Thailand. Once the trees stop producing sap, they're cut down and burned, which creates pollution.

Viraponsavan had an idea. What if he used the wood from old rubber trees in children's toys? Because wooden toys don't need to be as strong as wooden buildings, the strength of the wood doesn't matter. Repurposing the wood from rubber trees would both prevent pollution and save other trees. Viraponsavan founded PlanToys, one of the world's oldest and largest sustainable toy companies.

Once entrepreneurs have identified a problem and thought of a way to solve it, they consider how to turn that idea into a money-making business.

Drying wood makes it stronger, but can also involve using toxic chemicals. Viraponsavan teamed up with a local university to create a chemical-free wood drying process. This made the wood from rubber trees safe for use in children's toys.

Green Sense grows crops indoors under pink and blue LED lights and without the use of chemical fertilizers and pesticides.

For example, many farms are owned by international corporations and take up an enormous amount of land. American ecopreneur Robert Colangelo wondered, "What if farmers could grow more crops in less space? They wouldn't need as much land."

In 2013, Colangelo founded Green Sense Farms, where he grows crops indoors using artificial light. By stacking growing beds one on top of the other, he can grow more plants in less space. Pink and blue **LED** lights enable photosynthesis, allowing Colangelo to grow crops year-round.

Colangelo's indoor farm is environmentally friendly and profitable. Because his methods produce more plants per acre, he can grow and sell more crops with less expense. The farm is so unique and such a good use of space that in 2015, Green Sense partnered with a Chinese company called Star Global Holdings to build 20 similar farms in China.

*In the countryside, 90% of households in India cook by burning **biomass** such as wood or cow dung. In addition to creating air pollution, this practice leads to the destruction of forests and the risk of wildfires.*

2. Market Research

Market research looks at the buying habits of people of different ages and ethnicities, in various places. It also investigates what needs people have that aren't being filled by other businesses. This knowledge can lead to opportunities that help shape new companies and products.

In 2013, three university students in India were looking for an opportunity to put their engineering knowledge to use. Piyush Sohani, Koushik Yanamandram, and Shankar Ramakrishnan did market research by traveling through rural India. When they discovered that millions of Indians cooked on an open flame, they knew they had the perfect solution for a **market** that already existed. They founded SustainEarth Energy Solutions and developed GauGas. GauGas uses cow manure and other biodegradable products to create sustainable, clean-burning **biogas** for stoves and portable lights.

You make the call...

SustainEarth found a market no one else had reached. Brainstorm some potential markets in your community.

3. The Business Plan

SustainEarth identified their ultimate goal. They wanted to provide enough GauGas units to fill the cooking and lighting energy needs for 700 million rural Indians.

They outlined their **business plan**. Business plans include the following:

- short-term and long-term goals for the company
- a list of the obstacles and opportunities the company faces
- the company's financial needs
- strategies for the future

Creating this plan helped focus the company's business needs. SustainEarth's potential customers lived far from major cities. The company had to find organizations that could help them get in touch with these people, such as the Indian government's Departments of Agriculture and Animal Husbandry. The founders also needed start-up funds. They presented their business plan to a non-profit organization called Villgro, which provided them with money, expert advice, and support. The business plan allowed them to turn their idea into reality.

Koushik Yanamandram and Piyush Sohani of GauGas

GauGas units are miniature biogas factories. They are inexpensive and don't cause the environmental problems that burning wood does.

Finding Funds

4. Funding

Financing new ideas can be difficult, especially when they involve creating and testing new technologies. Development and testing can be expensive, and there is no guarantee of success. Some entrepreneurs use their own savings, others get a loan from family or a bank. You need a strong business plan to convince a bank to loan you money. If you do get a loan, you must pay it back with **interest**. Family loans do not always have interest attached to them, but paying family members back is vital, or it could cause hard feelings. Another way to get funding is through **crowdfunding** (see page 26).

Developing new methods of creating green energy is an example of how ideas can be costly to develop. Green energy is energy created in an environmentally friendly and sustainable way. This includes solar and wind power—but there's a catch.

Solar power can be generated only when it's sunny. Wind power works only when there's wind. But people use electricity all the time.

In 2010, Cameron Lewis figured out a way to store the extra energy created on extremely sunny or windy days so that it could be used any time. His invention uses the extra energy to power an air compressor. The compressor fills a heavy bag with air. The air-filled bag is stored under water.

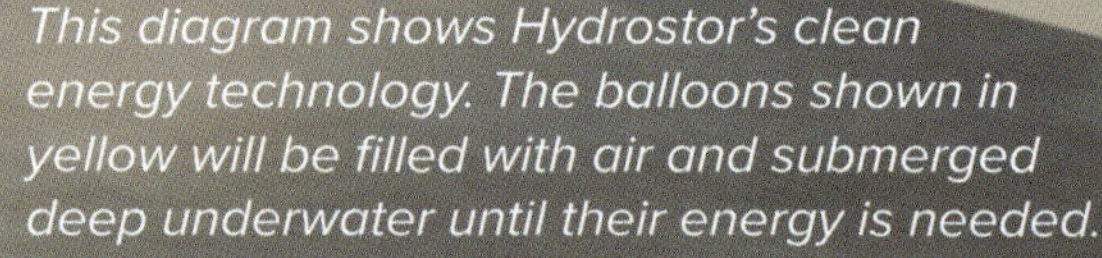

This diagram shows Hydrostor's clean energy technology. The balloons shown in yellow will be filled with air and submerged deep underwater until their energy is needed.

Hydrostor's air-balloon power system uses technology originally used in the airbags of jets.

When needed, the compressed air can power an underwater turbine to produce electricity. The idea sounds bizarre but is an effective way to create green electricity.

In order to test his idea, Lewis and his partner, Curtis van Wallegham, needed to build a prototype. A prototype is the first, imperfect version of a new technology. Developers test it to see what works and what needs improvement.

The pair started by using their own savings to start Hydrostor. Once their funds ran out, they looked for a group that would provide additional funds to help them improve their technology until it was good enough to sell. In 2013, Hydrostor received **venture capital** from ArcTern. ArcTern is a firm that invests large amounts of money in green start-ups in exchange for a share of the company.

Pablo Vidarte:
Electricity from Nature

Pablo Vidarte researched an inexpensive way to develop energy. In 2014, this young Spanish inventor founded Arkyne Technologies, a start-up company that developed Bioo Lite. This is a unique technology that connects a potted plant to nanowires, which are connected to a USB port. Bacteria in the pot break up the natural waste from photosynthesis and use it to produce electricity. You can plug your cellphone into your plant and recharge up to three times a day.

Before Bioo Lite, Vidarte had already founded two technology companies, including a geographical tracking firm named GEOO.

To pay for its prototype, Arkyne received funding from ***investors*** *that included the Spanish energy company Repsol.*

Crowdfunding

The needs of people in communities without electricity inspired Maurits Groen and Camille van Gestel to make a solar-powered light.

Crowdfunding is a way of raising money using the **Internet**. There are many crowdfunding websites, including Indiegogo, Kickstarter, and GreenUnite. Using them, people from around the world can read about a wide range of projects, choose one that interests them, and donate.

WakaWaka makes affordable gadgets that run on solar power. The company's most popular product is a solar light that gives off 80 hours of light after only eight hours in the sun. In 2012, Netherlands-based founders Maurits Groen and Camille van Gestel raised start-up funds for this venture through crowdfunding.

WakaWaka launched a fundraising campaign on Kickstarter. To encourage investment, the company offered free solar lamps to donors, gifts of solar lamps to schools without power in Kenya and Tanzania, and personal thank-you videos. Although the founders had a goal of $30,000, they managed to raise $48,399—a huge success.

In 2014, an outbreak of the Ebola virus struck the poor African nations of Sierra Leone and Liberia. Ebola is one of the most deadly diseases in the world. Between 2014 and the end of March 2016, the disease killed 3,590 people in Sierra Leone. To help medical staff fight this virus, WakaWaka launched another crowdfunding campaign. This time, they wanted to raise $5,000 to send free solar lights to health clinics affected by Ebola. The company offered rewards such as recipes for grilled cheese sandwiches and personal dinners with celebrity chef Eric Greenspan. It raised $8,890, which funded 10,000 solar lamps.

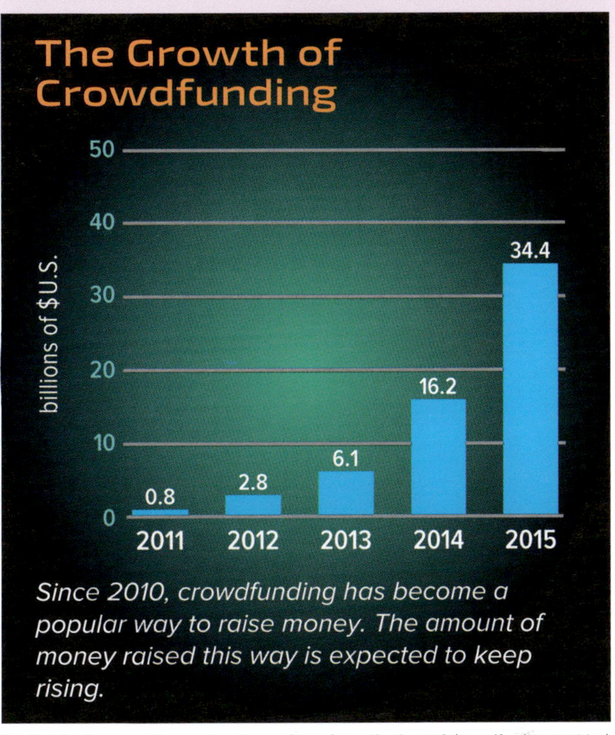

Since 2010, crowdfunding has become a popular way to raise money. The amount of money raised this way is expected to keep rising.

Credit: http://www.mylifecrowdfunding.org/home/crowdfunding-info/crowdfunding-statitisc/

In rural areas of Sierra Leone and Nigeria, the fuel for gas-powered generators used to power lights can be expensive and difficult to get. Solar-powered lamps helped make battling Ebola a little easier for health-care workers.

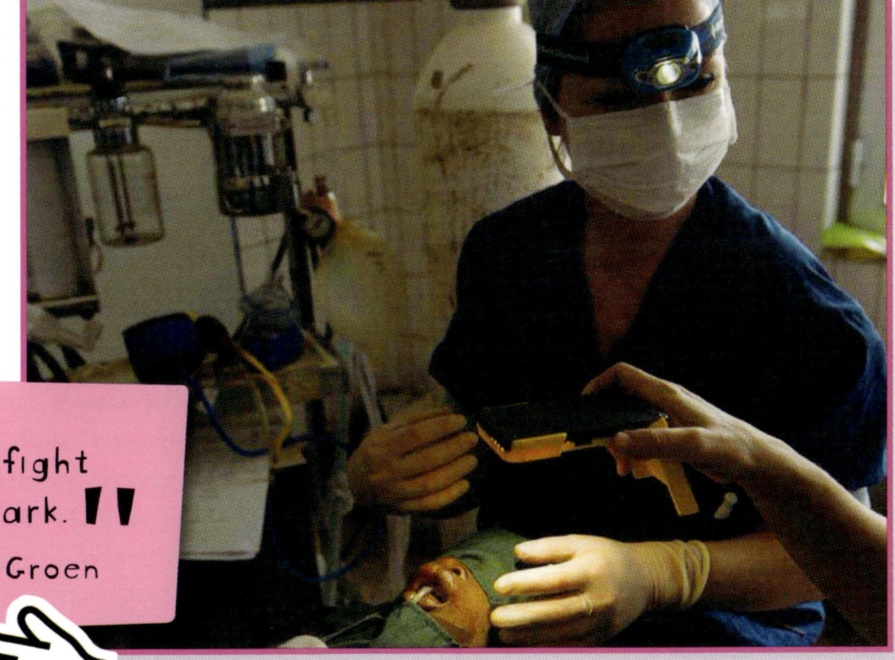

"You can't fight Ebola in the dark."
– Maurits Groen

Getting the Word Out

VALUES MATTER

THAT'S WHY ALL OF THE FRESH WILD-CAUGHT SEAFOOD WE SELL IS RATED FOR ITS ECOLOGICAL SUSTAINABILITY. IF IT DOESN'T MEASURE UP, WE DON'T SELL IT.

We work with independent ecological organizations that monitor sustainable fishing practices. And we were ranked #1 among U.S. supermarkets by Greenpeace for seafood sustainability.

All of the fresh wild seafood in our seafood departments is either rated sustainable by the **Marine Stewardship Council**, the world's leading certification program for sustainable seafood...

or it is rated green or yellow by **Monterey Bay Aquarium Seafood Watch** and the **Safina Center.**

From well-managed fisheries; caught in ways that cause little harm to habitats or other wildlife.

From fisheries where there are some concerns with how species are caught or managed.

We do not sell any red-rated wild seafood, including species found at other grocery stores.

WFM.COM/VALUESMATTER

America's Healthiest Grocery Store®

Whole Foods' ads encourage buyers to eat wholesome food that's good for them and the environment.

5. Marketing

The final step in the entrepreneurial process is marketing. Think of marketing as the voice of the product. There's no point in having a great idea if you have no way to communicate it. Good marketing provides a clear message to consumers. It includes direct advertising, such as television or radio commercials, giant billboards, and newspaper or magazine ads, and social media.

Whole Foods is a chain of stores that sell foods that are organically grown and don't contain any artificial additives, such as coloring or preservatives. The company makes sure that the meat it sells is raised organically and uses only fish caught in sustainable ways. It was founded in 1980 in Austin, Texas, by four natural food business owners—John Mackey, Craig Weller, Renee Hardy-Lawson, and Mark Skiles.

In 2014, the firm launched its first nationwide ad campaign. The campaign combined eye-catching photography with powerful wording that told consumers how doing good for the environment would benefit *them*. The ads sent a positive message about the stores' customers and their concern for the environment.

Rogan Gregory and Scott Hahn use similar methods to promote Loomstate, a sustainable clothing company they founded in 2003. Working out of Orlando, Florida, Loomstate finds independent growers of organic cotton. Instead of using direct advertising for its environmentally friendly cotton, the company started an Act Natural blog. The blog publishes photographs, articles, and other information about the company and what the founders believe. The blog is helping Loomstate build a loyal following of customers who are more likely to buy its products and will share the articles with their friends. This helps the company attract even more customers.

Millions of acres of land and billions of gallons of water are polluted each year by the chemical sprays used on traditional cotton farms. Loomstate's organic methods keep the water and soil clean and healthy.

Branding

Once a product has been developed, the next step is **branding**. A brand is more than a logo, name, or image. It also reflects the company's values, beliefs, and passion. Customers connect with a brand because they share these ideas.

Most handbags are made from leather from farmed animals, or from plastic. Luxury bag company Freedom of Animals was founded by American Morgan Bogle in 2013.

Bogle's purses and bags are made from recycled plastics and organic cotton. She describes her brand using just three words: *sustainable*, *ethical*, and *luxurious*. These words clearly communicate what the company believes and what kind of products consumers can expect.

Branding makes **marketing** easier. Having a strong brand ensures that the message sent to consumers is clear and consistent.

Freedom of Animals communicates its brand using simple and elegant advertisements. These create a sense of luxury and make the viewer feel content.

Branding also provides the creative direction of a company. University of Toronto students Gimmy Chu, Tom Rodinger, and Christian Yan founded the sustainable lighting company Nanoleaf. Their idea was to create a light bulb that is environmentally friendly, stylish, and beautiful.

Rodinger has a degree in biochemistry. Chu and Yan both studied Applied Science. Using their science backgrounds, they developed a geometrical light bulb that uses a fraction of the electricity of conventional bulbs. The design has made them a global leader in sustainable lighting. No wonder they define their brand as "Smarter by Design."

No entrepreneur works alone. The founders of Nanoleaf combined their unique talents.

Nanoleaf light bulbs use a unique 12-sided shape that delivers 360-degree lighting. It's Smarter by Design.

Tonya Kay: Eco-friendly Brand

Tonya Kay is a television actress and ecopreneur. In 2008 she founded Happy Mandible, an environmentally friendly vegan catering company that serves film studios. She understands that her company's way of doing business has to agree with its branding. That's why she has incorporated eco-friendly decisions into every aspect of her business. Kay has built a network of food suppliers who share her philosophy and use delivery trucks that run on clean-burning biogas.

Diversification

Smart marketing can include **diversification**. This refers to creating a range of different products or services to increase a business's chance of making money. Diversification allows companies to market to more people and sell a wider range of products or services.

In 2005, Greg Kiessling and Tom Heintzman founded Bullfrog Power, one of the oldest environmental entrepreneurship projects in Canada. Bullfrog Power provides green electricity to homes and businesses. It buys power from eco-friendly solar and wind farms. In 2016, more than 10,000 homes and 1,200 businesses across Canada used Bullfrog Power's green energy.

Bullfrog Power continues to grow by diversifying. Instead of just offering green electricity, the company has developed a range of products and services that increase its chances of success. In 2011, it began to offer green natural gas. Green natural gas comes from decaying organic matter, such as orange peels, egg shells, and grass clippings. When this natural material decomposes, an energy-rich gas is produced.

In 2015, Bullfrog Power released a line of green fuel to help businesses reduce the environmental impact of their transportation. The company's biodiesel is made from waste such as used cooking oils. Biodiesel is low in carbon emissions and better for the environment than regular gasoline.

Bullfrog Power provides consumers with a green energy choice. Customers pay their electrical company the usual price for electricity, and then pay Bullfrog Power to ensure that the same amount of green electricity is put onto the electrical grid on their behalf.

The company achieved success by appealing to green consumers and businesses. Users post its logo to show their support for green energy.

Bullfrog Power partnered with Chevrolet to encourage the development and use of electric cars. Buyers get two years of green electricity.

The company has also worked with Chevrolet Canada to develop the Chevrolet Volt, Bullfrog Power Edition. For a small fee, buyers get a Bullfrog Edition plaque and two years of enough green electricity to power their new electric car.

In addition, Bullfrog Power provides financial support to renewable energy projects like solar panels on schools. In 2015, it provided $125,000 to ZooShare, a cooperative that is building North America's first zoo-biogas plant. The plant will use manure and food waste from the Toronto Zoo to make biogas.

You make the call...

List 10 of your favorite brands and companies. Research one of these brands or companies. How did it start? Has it diversified? What are the advantages and disadvantages of such a move?

5 The Struggle for Success

Many entrepreneurs have good ideas that don't develop into successful businesses. In fact, 92% of all start-ups go out of business within three years. Many entrepreneurs, such as Mark Constantine, shown here, experience one or more failures before achieving success.

Millionaire Mark Constantine founded the cosmetic company Lush. His experience proves that while not all ideas lead to success, failure doesn't have to be the end.

Throughout the 1980s, Mark Constantine's England-based company, Constantine & Weir, made all-natural skin creams and soaps. In 1984, their largest customer, the Body Shop, realized that most of its best-selling products were coming from Constantine & Weir. The Body Shop couldn't risk having the smaller company decide to stop selling to them to become direct competitors. Such a move would have a disastrous effect by lowering the value of Body Shop shares. To prevent this, in 1985 the Body Shop paid about $8.6 million U.S. to buy Constantine & Weir. As part of the sale, Mark Constantine signed a contract promising not to start a competing cosmetic and skin-care store for five years.

Many Lush products use oil from moringa seeds, which grow in Africa. The company invests in local farming communities to create networks of healthy, eco-friendly farms.

So, instead of opening a store, Constantine and his wife Mo opened a mail-based company called Cosmetics-To-Go. The staff was so small that the company failed to keep up with orders. Soon they ran into trouble and had to sell the business in 1994 to pay off their debts.

In 1995, the Constantines started a new cosmetics company called Lush. Lush makes perfumes, soaps, and skin-care products without the use of animals. All its ingredients come from sustainable, independent farms. The company dehydrates its products, which allows it to use less packaging and reduces the amount of garbage sent to landfills. The packaging Lush does use is 100% recyclable. By 2016, the company had 900 stores in 49 countries around the world. The Constantines were worth $150 million.

"No issue is more important to the engineer, or entrepreneur, than intelligent failure."

— Dr. Jack V. Matson, Professor of Environmental Engineering

Five Successful Young Ecopreneurs

In recent years, many of the most promising green technologies have been developed by teens.

At age 19, Boyan Slat invented a way to remove plastic garbage from the ocean. He developed a V-shaped net and uses ocean currents to predict where the garbage will flow. The plastic is caught in his net, then pushed by the current into a tank. The tank can be lifted by crane onto a boat, emptied, and replaced.

Four Nigerian teens built a generator powered by urine. According to Duro-Aina Adebola, Akindele Abiola, Faleke Oluwatoyin, and Bello Eniola, the generator can provide six hours of electricity with just over 4 cups (1 liter) of pee. Though not yet ready for market, the generator is a great way to use natural waste to power low-income communities.

The generator works by separating hydrogen gas from the other contents of the urine. The hydrogen can then be used as a fuel.

Plastic reclaimed by Boyan Slat's The Ocean Cleanup can be recycled, or processed and turned into fuel.

In 2013, when he was 19, American ecopreneur Param Jaggi founded Ecoviate. Ecoviate is a software company that developed a phone app that provides users with the latest information and tips on environmentally friendly products. Users connect with each other creating a large network of people interested in saving the environment. Ecoviate has partnered with Trees for the Future. They plant one tree for every item sold or downloaded.

Umar donates the profits from Zee Bags to underprivileged children. Her dream is to make her city greener and to improve the living standard of her poor neighbors.

When she was six, Pakistan's Zymal Umar got the idea of using old newspapers to make recyclable shopping bags. She quickly made some bags at home and had soon sold hundreds under the company name Zee Bags. By the time she was nine, she was known around the world as one of the youngest ecopreneurs.

By 2016, Ecoviate's app had been downloaded more than 4,000 times. That's 4,000 new trees!

Azza Abdel Hamid Faiad was just 16 when she invented a new way to turn plastic into a clean-burning fuel. Unlike many other methods, hers doesn't produce harmful gases. She's currently working to get a **patent** before developing her idea further.

Faiad estimates that her method could create 138,000 tons (125,191 metric tons) of clean-burning fuel per year.

6 The Entrepreneur in You

Throughout this book, we've seen entrepreneurs from all walks of life. Though some of them have special skills, many of them are young people just like you.

Across North America, farmers make large round bales of hay and protect them from the weather using plastic wrap, shown here. YAY Bale replaces this plastic with a biodegradable wrap.

Entrepreneurs find opportunities in unlikely places. Some young students found such an opportunity in wrapped bales of hay.

The grade 8 and 9 students who invented YAY Bale call themselves the AVENGERS, A Very Energetic Nerdy Group of Environmentally Responsible Students. They plan to patent their invention.

A group of students at St. Thomas Aquinas High School in Russell, Ontario, Canada, discovered an entrepreneurial opportunity in their own neighborhood. Russell is in a farming area. When local farmers harvest fields of hay, they bale the grasses for animal feed and wrap the bales in eight to ten layers of plastic. Once used, the plastic usually ends up in landfills or burned, which produces greenhouse gases. Bothered by the waste, local students invented a fully biodegradable, eco-friendly bale wrap made from plant fibers.

Using sturdy, starchy plants like corn, they created a flexible sheet that works just like plastic wrap. Their **bioplastic** product is called YAY Bale. It can be broken down into an edible product or plowed back into the fields as fertilizer. Imagine taking the plastic you use to protect your hay and feeding it to your cows for dinner!

These young ecopreneurs didn't have access to millions of dollars. They worked in their science classes at school using the resources at hand. Their product is simple, effective, and good for the environment. More importantly, they solved a problem everyone else had overlooked.

You make the call...

Imagine what you can do to make a positive impact on the environment. Using the steps described in this book, make a plan to turn your idea into a money-making business.

Start Local

Students at Hamilton High School in Missoula, Montana, found a way to combine education with entrepreneurship. They grew a variety of fruits and vegetables in a school garden. In the process, they learned about soil preparation and plant care. They also learned how to harvest crops and prepare them for eating. In addition, they sold their produce at an annual market, which gained them marketing skills.

By participating in environmental entrepreneurship on a small, local level, these high-school students were able to develop new skills and make contacts. Whether or not they decide to start their own company, what they've learned from this experience will help them work with and for future entrepreneurs.

Working in a school vegetable garden is a great way to learn about nature. By selling the vegetables, you can connect with people interested in the environment.

Think Small, Dream Big

Small actions can have big consequences. Opportunities to apply entrepreneurial thinking don't have to change the entire world—just your own corner of it.

Remember phosphorus—that algae-growing chemical? In Bangor, Maine, high-school student Paige Brown invented a filter that can absorb and remove it from water. Although that may sound complicated, the filter is small and simple, and costs only $3 to make. Brown extracted a gel called "alginate" from a piece of seaweed and then mixed it with small pieces of aluminum and magnesium to make a gummy ball. She packed the balls inside an ordinary "jaw" hairclip and attached it to a piece of foam. The floating gadget absorbs phosphorus and helps make water healthier for animals.

Less Fuel
Less Pollution
Less Stress
More Carpool

Carma uses smartphone-based technology to arrange carpools. How might you develop something similar in your own community?

Today's ecopreneurs find inspiration everywhere. Carpooling can be a great way to reduce car exhaust, which contributes to global warming. In 2007, Irish entrepreneur Sean O'Sullivan founded Carma. His company collects money from customers for setting up carpools with people they may not know.

How are carpools arranged at your school or in your community? Is there a way to connect families who might not know each other?

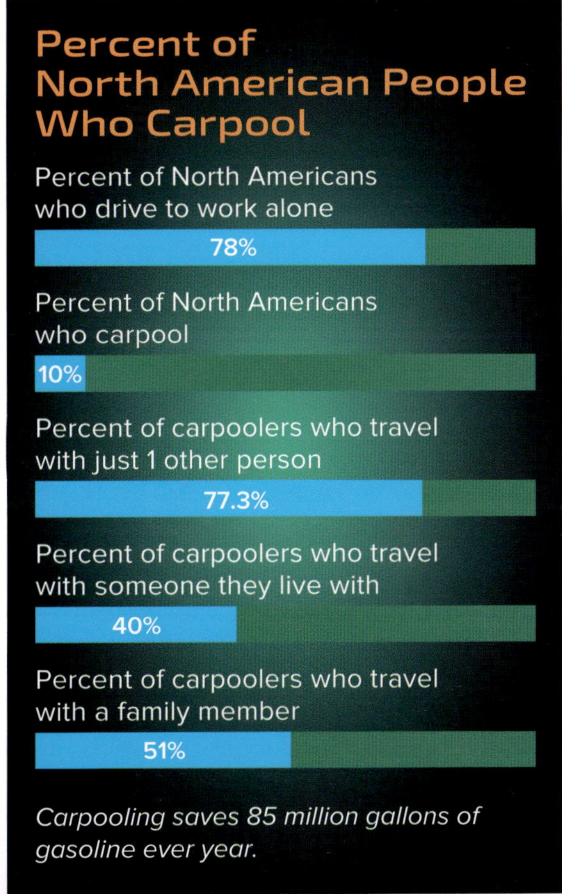

Credit: http://www.statisticbrain.com/carpool-statistics/

Future Opportunities

In the past 20 years, lowland gorilla populations in the Congo have declined by 77% due to human activities.

According to HSBC, one of the largest banks in the world, by the year 2020 ecopreneurs will be earning $2 trillion from solving climate-related problems. Some of these ecopreneurs are already working. Merhrdad Madjoubi, founder of Swedish Orbital Systems, learned that a 10-minute shower can use up to 20 gallons (76 liters) of water. Madjoubi developed a shower system that recycles water, thus cutting water consumption by 80% to 95%.

Other opportunities can be found—literally—in the palm of your hand. Smartphones and tablets rely on a mineral called coltan, which is mined in the African nation of Congo. These mining activities destroy the habitat of endangered species such as lowland gorillas. This is a problem that has yet to be solved. But for an entrepreneur, problems are actually opportunities. As the 21st century moves forward, ecopreneurs will find creative solutions for this and other problems. What other opportunities might be waiting for an entrepreneurial spirit—like yours?

"Be the change you wish to see in the world."

– Mohandas K. (Mahatma) Gandhi, Civil rights leader in India

Think About It

1. All entrepreneurs make mistakes and have to deal with failure. How do you handle mistakes and failures? How can you learn from them in order to succeed in the future?
2. Ecopreneurs are passionate about the environment. What interests you about protecting the environment? What problem would you like to solve?
3. Entrepreneurs come up with creative solutions to everyday problems. Describe a time when you thought of a unique or creative way to solve a problem in your own life.
4. Name five activities in which you are needlessly wasteful. Consider how you get to school, what you buy from the grocery store, etc. What can you do to reduce the waste you produce?
5. Successful entrepreneurs surround themselves with people who can help them achieve their goals. Are there people with whom you work well? How can you work together to solve a problem or start a small business?
6. Knowing your strengths is important when thinking about the kind of business you want to run. What are you good at? How might that help you develop a business?

Next Steps

If you think the path of an ecopreneur is right for you, here are some things you can do to get started:

- Try growing a vegetable garden at home or at school. This is a great way to learn about how food is grown and how we can use nature to make something useful. You might even sell what you grow!
- Join a community group that's working on environmental issues. Volunteer to help. Working with like-minded people might spark an idea for an ecopreneurial venture.
- Read books about the environment and green businesses. Learn about what people in the past have done. Consider how you might improve on some of these ideas.

Founded by Liansheng Mao in 1998, Yingli Solar is the world's largest solar panel manufacturer. It ships to more than 90 countries around the world.

Bibliography / Sources

Books

Cooney, Scott. *Build a Green Small Business.* McGraw-Hill, 2008.

Croston, Glen. *Starting Green.* Entrepreneur Media Inc., 2009.

Ferriss, Tim. *The 4-Hour Workweek.* Crown Publishing Group, 2007.

Hawken, Paul, Amory Lovins, and L. Hunter Lovins. *Natural Capitalism: Creating the Next Industrial Revolution.* Little, Brown and Company, 1999.

Websites

www.bioo.tech

www.blackenterprise.com

www.designindaba.com/articles/creative-work/gau-gas-creates-energy-animal-waste

www.e2.org

www.forbes.com

www.greenoptimistic.com/teenagers-top-green-inventions/#.VyfN6ISDFBc

www.instructables.com/id/-Electricity-Generating-Footwear

www.kickstarter.com

www.nanoleaf.me

www.usnews.com/opinion/blogs/world-report/2014/09/18/china-is-besting-the-us-on-renewable-energy

www.wired.com

http://ecopreneurist.com

http://ideas.ted.com/entrepreneur-avani-singh-ummeed

http://ted.com

http://thetab.com/us/harvard/2015/12/24/is-deepika-kurup-the-most-talented-freshman-at-harvard-2016

https://ideamensch.com/26-green-entrepreneurs/

Learning More

Books to Read

Bernstein, Daryl. *Better Than a Lemonade Stand: Small Business Ideas for Kids*. Aladdin. 2012.

Cooney, Scott. *Build a Green Small Business*. McGraw-Hill, 2008.

Covey, Sean. *The 7 Habits of Highly Effective Teens*. Simon & Schuster. 2014.

Croston, Glen. *Starting Green*. Entrepreneur Media Inc., 2009.

Funk, Mckenzie. *Windfall: The Booming Business of Global Warming*. Penguin. 2015.

Hoogeveen, Margaret. *What Is Social Entrepreneurship?* (Your Start-Up Starts Now!) Crabtree Publishing, 2016.

Hyde, Natalie. *What Is Entrepreneurship?* (Your Start-Up Starts Now!) Crabtree Publishing, 2016.

Mason, Helen. *What Is Digital Entrepreneurship?* (Your Start-Up Starts Now!) Crabtree Publishing, 2016.

Websites

www.bioconstruct.com/how-does-a-biogas-plant-work

Learn how a biogas plant creates electricity.

www.ted.com/talks/donald_sadoway_the_missing_link_to_renewable_energy?language=en

An expert from the Massachusetts Institute of Technology explains why solar and wind power haven't caught on like coal and oil, and reveals a big opportunity for future ecopreneurs.

Videos:

http://tedxtalks.ted.com/video/The-Making-of-A-Young-Entrepren

At just 11 years old, Gabrielle Jordan Williams started her own jewelry business. In this video, she tells her story and gives advice to other young entrepreneurs.

www.ted.com/talks/maya_penn_meet_a_young_entrepreneur_cartoonist_designer_activist?language=en

At just 13, Maya Penn is a cartoonist, designer, environmental activist. She also owns her own eco-friendly clothing company. Learn about her unique story, and the steps she took to success.

Glossary

biogas Gas produced by the natural breakdown of organic material, such as plant or food waste or sewage

biomass Any material that comes from living or once-living things

bioplastic Plastic made from organic materials, such as vegetable fats and oils

branding Marketing strategy that combines a company's name, logo, and values to create a cohesive message

business plan Planning document that includes all aspects of a business; used to assess whether a business will work and to get financing

carbon dioxide (CO_2) Gas produced through burning and other natural processes

climate change Long-term change in weather patterns that can lead to increased floods, droughts, and fierce storms

consumers Buyers

crowdfunding Raising money online from a large number of people

decompose Rot or decay

digital entrepreneurs Business people who use online or other electronic media for all or part of their business

diversification Creating a range of different products or services to increase a business's chance of making money

ecopreneurs People who start a business that solves an environmental issue

entrepreneur Person who starts a business based on their idea

entrepreneurial process Steps that entrepreneurs take, including idea, vision, research, planning, team building, and marketing

entrepreneurship The process of turning an idea into a business

environmental entrepreneurship Starting a business by combining concern for the environment with sound business practices

global warming Increase of Earth's average temperature due to human activities (see also "greenhouse gases")

green Environmentally friendly; eco-friendly

greenhouse gases Gases, including carbon dioxide and methane, that trap heat from the Sun in Earth's atmosphere and increase the average global temperature

income Money earned from the sale of a product or service, or through employment

innovative Describing something or someone that uses ideas or methods

interest Fee paid for the use of someone's money, usually a percentage of the amount owed

Internet Global network that connects millions of computers for the exchange of information

investors People who give money to for-profit enterprises with the expectation of a financial return

LED Stands for "light-emitting diodes." Lights or light bulbs that use this technology convert energy directly into light without producing the heat that conventional bulbs create.

market People interested in paying for a product or service

marketing Advertising and promoting a product or service

methane One of the greenhouse gases

organic Refers to farming and growing crops with natural instead of chemical fertilizers or pesticides

patent Government license granting ownership of an idea or invention

phosphorus Chemical that contributes to plant growth

photosynthesis Process through which plants make energy using sunlight, carbon dioxide, and water; the byproducts of this process are oxygen and certain carbohydrates

profit Amount of money left over after a company's expenses have been subtracted from its total revenue

start-up (*n*) a new business; (*adj*) relating to the starting of a new business

start-up funds Money necessary to keep a new business going until it becomes profitable

sustainable Refers to a system, product, or technique that can exist without doing damage to the environment; eco-friendly; green

vendor A seller

venture capital Money invested in a start-up business, usually in exchange for some partial ownership of the company

wind farm Area of land with many wind turbines producing large amounts of electrical energy

Index

Author Biography

Alexander Offord is the author of three books for young readers. He is also an award-winning playwright and director, and co-founder of the highly acclaimed avant-garde theatre company, Good Old Neon. During his time as an independent artist, he has become involved with several environmental and social justice groups. He lives in Toronto with his partner, Nicole, and their wire-haired dachshund.